STANLEY HOFFMANN

AMERICA GOES -BACKWARD

NEW YORK REVIEW BOOKS, NEW YORK

THIS IS A NEW YORK REVIEW BOOK

PUBLISHED BY THE NEW YORK REVIEW OF BOOKS

AMERICA GOES BACKWARD

by Stanley Hoffmann

This edition published in 2004 in the United States of America by
The New York Review of Books, 1755 Broadway, New York, NY 10019
www.nyrb.com

Book and cover design by Milton Glaser, Inc.

A catalog record for this book is available from the Library of Congress

ISBN 1-59017-156-X

Printed in the United States of America on acid-free paper.

November 2004

1 3 5 7 9 10 8 6 4 2

CONTENTS

FOREWORD

THIS ESSAY HAS BEEN WRITTEN OVER A PERIOD OF SIXTEEN MONTHS. Part One was first published in *The New York Review* of June 12, 2003. I have not revised it, for the simple reason that I found, alas, nothing to change in it. Part Two was written in July–August 2004.

I have spent much of my time as a scholar and teacher studying American foreign policy, from the perspective of a Frenchman (whose mentor in international relations had been Raymond Aron) living in the United States, as a citizen of the US as well as of France, and troubled by the way both the American study of international relations and US foreign policy have displayed a tendency toward America-centeredness that has been detrimental to both, despite the great strides forward accomplished by the former and the many successes of the latter. My criticism of, and indignation at, the war in Iraq echo my feelings and analysis of the Vietnam War, and express my worries about the direction taken by the American nation under the administration of George W. Bush.

—STANLEY HOFFMANN

AMERICA
GOES
-BACK
WARD

As published in *The New York Review of Books*
June 12, 2003

AMERICA GOES BACKWARD

LESS THAN TWO AND A HALF YEARS AFTER it came to power, the Bush administration, elected by fewer than half of the voters, has an impressive but depressing record. It has, in self-defense, declared one war—the war on terrorism—that has no end in sight. It has started, and won, two other wars. It has drastically changed the strategic doctrine and the diplomatic position of the United States, arguing that the nation's previous positions were obsolete and that the US has enough power to do pretty much as it pleases. At home, as part of the war on terrorism, it has curbed civil liberties, the rights of refugees and asylum seekers, and the access of foreign students to US schools and universities. It holds in custody an unknown number of aliens and some Americans treated as "enemy combatants," suspected but not indicted, whose access to hearings and lawyers has been denied. The Republican majority in both houses of Congress and the courts' acceptance of the notion that the

President's war powers override all other concerns have given him effective control of all the branches of government. The administration's nominees to the courts would consolidate its domination of the judiciary.

The Justice Department is also supporting efforts to have the Supreme Court reverse its previous decisions on affirmative action and on women's rights. The social programs that have softened the harshness of capitalism since the New Deal, inferior as they are to those of other liberal democracies, are threatened by the Republicans' relentless war against the state's welfare functions, their preference for voluntary over mandated solutions to health care, and for private over public schools. Large numbers of old, sick, or very young people, mainly among the poor, will be deprived of financial assistance as the result of administration policies. Those policies include the cuts that will result from the huge deficits caused by military expenditures and reduced taxes and revenues, and the gradual transfer of many welfare and educational costs to states that are broke, must balance their budgets, and receive little aid from the federal government.

The political forces that many expected to question policies and express dissent have been remarkably meek and
mute. The Democrats are reluctant to attack a popular president. Before the war against Iraq and during the war itself,
the press and television gave Bush the benefit of the doubt,
with chauvinistic support being offered under the guise of
patriotism. Anyone who tunes into BBC radio and television can only be struck by the contrast in style and substance between its news programs and those on the
American networks. (In no US newspaper or broadcast that
I have seen has the French position on Iraq been accurately
presented.[1]) It sometimes seemed that the press had
become "embedded" not only in the fighting forces but in
Washington officialdom itself.

The US remains a liberal democracy, but those who have
hoped for progressive policies at home and enlightened
policies abroad may be forgiven if they have become
deeply discouraged by a not-so-benign soft imperialism,
by a fiscal and social policy that takes good care of the
rich but shuns the poor on grounds of a far from

"compassionate conservatism," and by the conformism, both dictated by the administration and often spontaneous among the public, that Tocqueville observed 130 years ago. Some will say that it could have been worse; but a blunter form of domination might have resulted in sharper and more organized opposition.

The administration has proceeded more stealthily. Welfare cuts can be blamed on the states. The lopsided tax cuts are misleadingly presented as benefiting us all. Shrinking environmental protection can be justified as a defense of the economy. Increased surveillance of citizens' private activities and of aliens' movements are said to be "required" by homeland security. A military budget equal to those of all other nations combined can be justified by the vulnerability of the US revealed on September 11, and by the proliferation of threats. Every decision or move can be defended in reassuring language. The public is invited both to take pride in America's unique might and to worry about the perils that lurk everywhere.

Indeed, a technique that the administration has used

brilliantly is the manipulation of fear. Americans have been "shocked and awed" by September 11, and the President has found in this criminal act not just a rationale, hitherto missing, for his administration, but a lever he could use to increase his, and his country's, power. All that was needed was, first, to proclaim that we were at war (something other societies attacked by terrorists have not done), second, to extend that war to states sheltering or aiding terrorist groups, and third, to allege connections between Islamist terrorists and "rogue states," such as Iraq and Iran, engaged in efforts to obtain or build weapons of mass terror. When, a few days before the war on Iraq began, the President several times linked Saddam Hussein and al-Qaeda at a press conference, not one of the sixteen journalists who asked questions about Iraq challenged him.

The case against Iraq's regime was at first based on stoking American fears about hidden weapons of mass destruction (while downplaying fears that North Korean nuclear bombs might provoke). When it became clear that Saddam Hussein's ability to threaten American security had been much exaggerated since the weapons proved hard to find, and the possession by Iraq of nuclear weapons was effectively denied by the UN inspectors, the reason for the war was shifted to human rights and democracy.

Another technique was a resort to Orwellian rhetoric. The President told Americans that the war was not a policy chosen among others, but a necessity imposed by Saddam. Nations that resisted the administration's rush to war were presented as hostile for reasons of greed or of an incurable anti-Americanism. Colin Powell stated that Jacques Chirac had said that France wouldn't go to war against Iraq "under any circumstances." In fact, as Powell must have known, and as I have been told on very good authority, the French President had earmarked French forces for war if the inspectors, after a limited number of weeks and after having followed a series of "benchmarks" not dissimilar from those Tony Blair had demanded, concluded that Iraq did have forbidden weapons and could not be disarmed peacefully. French diplomacy could be faulted for not making its positions clearer; but Chirac's statement referred only to the text of the second resolution drafted by the US and Britain for submission to the Security Council, and then withdrawn. On March 16, after the US turned down Chirac's proposal to consider using force if the inspectors reached an impasse in Iraq in thirty days, he told Christiane Amanpour on 60 Minutes that if "our strategy, inspections, were failing, we would consider all the options, including war." Equally Orwellian on the part of the US was the talk about "the coalition," used even when a military move was made only by US forces.

2.

ONE ASPECT OF THE WRECKING OPERATION that the administration has undertaken is worth special attention—the destruction of some of the main schemes of cooperation that have been established since 1945 and are aimed at introducing some order and moderation into the jungle of traditional international conflicts. In order to remove Saddam Hussein from power before the weather became too hot, and to replace a policy of containment of Iraq that had, after 1991, worked reasonably well[2] with the policy of preventive war projected in the national security doctrine published in September 2002, the US did not hesitate to do the following:

1. It indicated bluntly that it might act unilaterally, on the basis of much earlier UN resolutions, which demanded proof of the destruction of weapons of mass destruction. Only pressure from Tony Blair led Bush to abandon this course, while Bush also made it clear that he distrusted UN inspectors. Resolution 1441, adopted unanimously in November after weeks of negotiations, was, not unexpectedly, sufficiently vague to allow both the Americans and

the French to believe that they had prevailed. When, on British insistence, the US introduced in March a second resolution promising war despite the reports of the UN inspectors' evidence of some progress toward compliance, the administration resorted to a crude display of threats and inducements aimed at obtaining the nine votes needed for the resolution to pass. When it became clear that those votes could not be secured and the text would be vetoed by France and Russia, the US withdrew it, went to war, denounced the UN as a failure comparable to the League of Nations, and made no effort to repair the breach: the UN had not been "with us," and thus it was "against us."

2. The US split NATO in order to isolate the French and the Germans, provoking both countries by asking for NATO military assistance to Turkey that the Turks themselves had not solicited. The US obtained this aid through the Military Committee of NATO, of which France is not a member. The US then left NATO—which had been so useful to the US in Kosovo—on the sidelines.

3. The US engaged, along with Blair, in an effort to divide the European Union by obtaining the signatures for a statement in support of the US by leaders of several long-standing members and most of the new Eastern European members. As a result, the attempt at shaping a common foreign and security policy for the EU, undertaken in 1998, collapsed.[3]

This disdain for international institutions, and adoption of a strategic doctrine that gives a prominent place to pre-emptive war in violation of the provisions of the UN Charter, along with the decision to go to war without the support of the Security Council required by the charter, are all part of a tough new policy of US predominance whose implications are extremely serious but remain largely unexamined.[4]

Defenders of Bush's policy look at international organizations as unacceptable if they constrain US national interests. As for international law, it is seen as little more than words on paper, unless it is backed by force. For the Bush administration, functional institutions such as UNAID have their merits in dealing with technical needs; but the UN's political institutions, far from providing justification for the resort to force according to the rules of the UN Charter, are seen as on trial and are usually found wanting.[5] In the case of Iraq, the administration's claims of the UN's inadequacy were based on its failure, after 1991, to obtain Saddam Hussein's disarmament, and its failure to act to prevent a terrible tyranny from committing vast crimes against its subjects.

The defenders of Bush's post–September 11 policy present it, by contrast, as a realistic evaluation of a world still based on the principle of national sovereignty. Only states have power, and are or can be held accountable for their acts (hence, for example, the Bush administration's rejection of the International Criminal Court). In the special case of the US, it holds its Constitution and domestic laws superior to international law and particularly to supranational rules of the kind the members of the EU have accepted. The problem is, of course, that, as a result, the UN is condemned both for its incapacity to decide or to enforce its decisions and for its occasional attempts to put restraints on the actions of its members. In the case of Iraq, the two UN failures I have mentioned were actually those of the member states.

Pushing aside the UN, or refusing to accept curbs on the use of US force, can mean one of two things. The US may want to return to pre-1914 conditions, when the only international limitations on the right of each sovereign state to use force were rules dealing with the *jus in bello*— the ways in which force could be used—but not with the goals. This discards the progress accomplished in trying to form a modern *jus ad bellum*, a definition of the purposes for which force can legitimately be used (self-defense, collective security) and of the procedures that can authorize the resort to force. Treaties such as the genocide convention and international tribunals created to judge persons responsible for crimes against humanity or war crimes would be discarded. The post-1945 efforts to protect the human rights of individuals against states would also be scrapped. Security in the world jungle would depend exclusively on an efficiently functioning balance of power, or on voluntary self-restraint by a dominant superpower.

Or else the US, seeing itself as the guardian of world order, would leave restraints on other states standing (unless they are its allies), and reserve to itself the right to select those restraints of international law and institutions that serve its interests and to reject all the others. President Bush, in telling others what the US "expects" of them, is coming very close to that position.

It is sad to have to remind those who endorse such positions that in a world consisting of almost two hundred states of very uneven strength and cohesion, and where the many forms of interdependence reduce the actual sovereignty of all, a pure and simple return to the rule of the strongest would be a catastrophic regression. It would promote insecurity, not security or moderation. Those who approved of the war in Iraq for entirely understandable reasons of humanitarianism, of pity for the Iraqi people, and of horror at Saddam Hussein's regime seldom considered that a precedent used for a "good" cause can easily be used by others for causes they would object to: Russia could use it against Georgia, India against Pakistan, North Korea against South Korea.

It is true that international law and the UN Charter are full of flaws, are not self-executing, and are used frequently as fig leaves for the naked expression of power. But all laws and all institutions exist in a kind of limbo, between the ideals they express and the daily transactions among the passions and interests they seek to control. In world affairs, devoid of central power, of a strong judiciary, of a world police, the gulf between the two is wider than within most states. This is a reason for trying to close it, to persuade states to change their definition of their own interests, to extend and deepen the range of their ideals. A legal code that would merely ratify what people do, and not codify what they ought to do, would be a bad joke.

Actually, as the American scholar David C. Hendrickson reminds us, most international legal and ethical norms are "also prudential in character," and often simply register "the lessons of experience."[6] Observing them is in the interest of the US because the responsibility for world order cannot be carried by the US alone. The task would exceed the capacities of the US, despite its huge military forces. "Observance of basic principles of the law of nations, together with action within the constraints of an international consensus," Hendrickson writes, "are two basic ways in which the United States has acquired such legitimacy as it now enjoys in the international system."

Recent US doctrines and actions have damaged that legitimacy, a damage compounded by a contemptuous attitude even toward NATO, and toward allies that have disagreed with US tactics or with the US evaluation of the consequences of a war in Iraq. The language of "you're either with us or against us," of punishments and rewards, sounds imperious (and imperial). It is likely to be counterproductive in the long term: as the former US diplomat John Brady Kiesling has written, "the more aggressively we use our power to intimidate our foes, the more foes we create and the more we validate terrorism as the only effective weapon of the powerless against the powerful."[7] One of the many impulses behind the unprecedented antiwar demonstrations throughout the world by people of all ages and classes was to protest an American policy that gives to its military might, and threats to use it, pride of place among all the kinds of power it has at its disposal.

DURING THE COLD WAR THE US LAPSED into unilateral sponsorship
of violence in Southeast Asia, the Middle East, and Latin
America; but in the main contest with the USSR it showed
itself aware of the advantages that regional and global
cooperation provide to the dominant power. International
cooperation had the benefits of lightening the military and
financial burdens of the US as well as giving it more influence and providing ways of monitoring and shaping the
behavior of others. The alternative is a policy of hubris, in
which international domination is presented under the
mask of universal benign ideals. Such domination will cer-
tainly incite some enemies either to resort to terrorism or
to obtain weapons of mass destruction, so as to avoid
being crushed in conventional wars.

The choice between unilateralism and international
cooperation will, in the near future, have to be made with
respect to four challenges that the US faces. The first is the
challenge of creating a workable Iraqi society and polity.
The US has done a huge service to the Iraqi people by
removing a sadistic dictatorship. But the lack of American

3.

preparation for the tasks that follow, in contrast with the preparation for war, has been shocking. US hopes of being greeted enthusiastically by Iraqis as liberators have been undermined by a familiar tendency to underestimate the depth of "native" nationalism (as in South Vietnam),[8] by the failure to protect hospitals, the national museum and library, and other public buildings from looting (whereas American soldiers immediately protected the Oil Ministry), and by the failure to improve living conditions in the first phase of occupation.

Moreover, the early decision to entrust the reshaping of Iraq to the Pentagon not only confirmed the decisive role in foreign policy that the Defense Department had begun to play during the Clinton years but concealed the very different interests and concerns that are manifest in the administration. In the Defense Department, the civilian coterie of neoconservatives and hard-line pro-Israeli hawks has promoted a grandiose fantasy of using Iraq as the model for democratizing the Muslim world. This assumes that liberal democracy, pro-Americanism, and Arab moderation in dealing with Israel can all be obtained at the same time, and that nationalist, populist, and religious impulses won't result in anti-Americanism and in even greater hostility toward Israel.

At best, the task would be long and hard, and require a long US stay in Iraq. Indeed, if Arab and Iranian rulers should embrace liberal reforms, it would be because of internal pressures, not because of democratic winds originating in Iraq and fanned by the US. Rumsfeld has in the past supported the views of his deputies and advisers, but his enthusiasm for a long military occupation appears very limited. Before Paul Bremer was announced as the new US proconsul on May 6, 2003, the Pentagon's appointee in Iraq, retired general Jay Garner, favored Kurdish representatives and ex–Iraqi exiles as rulers of the country. With Garner now departing, the State Department and the CIA have their own favorites. All of them will ultimately have to choose between Iraq as a protectorate and Iraq as a self-determining country, which may or may not be democratic; America's protégés in the Gulf and Egypt are anything but democracies.

In view of signs of Iraqi resentment of a protracted occupation, the American government may be tempted to keep it short, but the risks of chaos are great, especially if power is transferred to former Iraqi exiles with little support among the people. America has no easy choices. Should the US encourage all political and religious factions to assert themselves and to claim a share of power? This would sacrifice both effective governance and the chances of liberalism to achieve representativeness. Should it exclude groups deemed illiberal or intolerant, thus sacrificing representation to its own preferences and driving the excluded further into radical and anti-American positions?[9]

Such considerations underline the US interest in turning for help to others with more involvement in "nation-building": to the UN, with its experience in the Balkans and East Timor, and to the EU and NATO, with their records in Kosovo and in Afghanistan. This would be helpful to the US in many ways: for peacekeeping, for administrative supervision, for sharing costs and political burdens. Such organizations could provide a fairer distribution of reconstruction contracts and a more impartial control of oil revenues than the US. If the US chooses to retain power over all these matters while relegating the UN to a fuzzy "coordinating" role, as could be the case under the recent US draft resolution, the hostility and suspicions it encounters in the Arab world could rise.

The second problem is as urgent as ever: peace between Israel and the Palestinians. The administration's obsession with Iraq, the hawks' conviction that the balance of forces between Israel and the Arabs would change in Israel's favor if Iraq were first "liberated," the President's dislike of Yasser Arafat and dismay at the terrorism of suicide bombers—all these resulted in a postponement of American attempts to revive a peace process. Pressure from Tony Blair and from Colin Powell, and America's current predominance in the Middle East, have led to the installation of Abu Mazen as Palestinian prime minister and the release of a "road map." Few deny that ordinary Arabs as well as officials in palaces or ministries have been deeply disappointed by American delays and partiality toward Ariel Sharon, and by what they have seen as a double standard in the enforcement of UN resolutions. What remains to be shown is the will of the US to become, as was the case with Clinton in 2000, the chief force working for a fair settlement.

If the US delays again or leaves the bargaining to the parties, the Arabs' sense of injustice and humiliation will grow. Combined with present misgivings among Muslims about the American war in Iraq, this might lead to more successes for fundamentalists, and to greater numbers of terrorists. The leadership of Abu Mazen may be an improvement over that of Arafat, but the gap between Palestinians and Israelis is much deeper than it was in 2000. Sharon seems unlikely to make as many concessions as Ehud Barak did. The problems of the settlements, Jerusalem, and the right of return are at least as difficult as ever. The powerful hard-line pro-Israel supporters in the White House, the Defense Department, and Congress may demand that before negotiations begin the new Palestinian government not only try energetically to curb terrorism, but give priority to obtaining a decisive success in a possibly bloody policy of antiterrorism.

In view of these lopsided pressures in and on the US, an American government concerned with its relations with the Arab world would be well advised to encourage the participation of the other coauthors of the "road map": the EU, Russia, and the UN. Sharon views all these with deep distrust. Unilateralists and pro-Israel lobbyists, inside and outside the administration, would object. But if the US would end its monopoly on being the mediator between the two parties it would go far toward appeasing an old grievance of the allies of the US and of the members of the UN.

The third issue, nuclear policy, has been pushed to the forefront by the new American strategic doctrine. In US rhetoric, weapons of mass destruction in hostile hands have become a potential *casus belli*. The administration says it fears that waiting until its foes already have nuclear bombs may allow them to deter the US and make American deterrence impossible—a fear that nothing in our past experience with the USSR and China justifies. The current doctrine encourages American officials to envisage taking preventive action before nuclear and other weapons of mass destruction are produced. A policy of endorsing preventive threats and strikes is being put in place.

This is a doubly dangerous approach. First, nuclear weapons are far more formidable than biological and chemical ones, and far more detectable. Chemical and biological programs are difficult to prevent but it is not impossible to neutralize their effects.[10] Second, American unilateral preventive action against states that try to acquire a nuclear arsenal would encourage other states to do the same in order to protect against countries they consider to be their foes—once again, a recipe for turning the world into a jungle. On the other hand, the experience with sanctions against states alleged to have such weapons— whether the sanctions are sponsored by the UN or the US—has been disappointing, sometimes less damaging to a targeted government than to its citizens. There is no substitute for a policy of concerted diplomatic pressure exerted by the UN and of collective, and selective, measures of coercion. These range from much stronger international controls on imported technologies to more intrusive inspections than in the past. They could ultimately include the use of force under international auspices against nuclear power plants that are being built or operated. This means a reinforcement, not—as Bush proposes—a repudiation, of the present nuclear nonproliferation regime.

Finally, the case of Saddam Hussein has raised the difficult issue of international action against regimes that pursue policies of ferocious repression of the opposition, real or suspected. Here international law has failed, and the UN has legitimized only limited interventions. International law and the UN Charter ban armed interventions in the domestic affairs of states. This was one of the grounds of the policy of nonintervention followed by the US under Bush senior in 1991, when Saddam Hussein savagely crushed the groups the US had encouraged to revolt. Soon after, the US supported collective interventions to protect the Kurds from further massacres by the Saddam Hussein regime (which made Kurdish autonomy within

Iraq possible), to stop the chaos and famine in Somalia (a fiasco), and to prevent massacres on ethnic grounds (in Bosnia, very late, and in Kosovo and East Timor). No such intervention took place in the biggest case of genocide, Rwanda, where the UN and the US behaved equally badly.[11] In Kosovo, the Security Council, despite the formal requirements of the UN Charter, was ignored because Russian and Chinese vetoes were certain; the US and its European allies used NATO to legitimize their action (and the Security Council and the secretary-general refused to condemn it). Thus a new norm was established: collective intervention against a government committing serious human rights violations could be justified, especially when these violations threaten regional or international peace and security.

None of these cases entailed "regime change." To limit a state's sovereignty by collective intervention against its government's assault on human rights is one thing; to forcibly remove a government and replace it with one more acceptable to the interveners is a far more radical attack on sovereignty. The US was passive when Saddam Hussein gassed the Kurds in the 1980s, and killed Kurds and Shiites in large numbers in 1991; it never raised in the UN the issue of regime change on human rights grounds. When this issue became, in the US and Britain, the most effective argument for war, humanitarians and liberals were split. For some, the demise of an evil regime was what mattered most, although they were often worried about American intentions. Others, who were equally troubled by Saddam Hussein's terror, were unwilling to approve of a unilateral American attack, especially since it opened the way for other countries to change whatever regimes they claimed were guilty of atrocities. They plausibly argued that, thanks in part to the presence of US troops in the region, the US could have worked out a multilateral consensus for continuing inspections and for disarmament, but refused to do so.

The issue of humanitarian intervention for "regime change" has now been raised, and we cannot push it back into the bottle by deliberately avoiding it. But it is not an issue the UN is likely to deal with effectively. Too many states among UN members have bloody domestic records, and they can be expected to block any proposal for a forcible collective intervention to change a regime.

What would be needed would be a new, two-stage system: (1) a group of UN members would ask the Security Council to authorize collective intervention to overthrow an evil regime, one clearly responsible for atrocities; (2) if the Security Council refuses or is unable to act, an appeal would be made to a new institution: an Association of Democratic Nations that would, in addition to members of NATO, be made up of Asian, African, and Latin American liberal democracies, such as India, South Africa, and Chile, as well as Australia and New Zealand. Only liberal democracies would be admitted as members.

If such an association approved a collective intervention to change a regime, it would report its reasons and its decisions to the secretary-general of the UN, and could proceed to act. Such an Association of Democratic Nations could also provide useful advice to new democracies, and bring before the International Criminal Court or a special international court military or civilian leaders involved in crimes against humanity, war crimes, or genocide. Alas, the Bush administration cannot be expected to try to work out such a needed reform.

Too often, this administration has given, to many Americans and even more to foreigners, the impression that it is drunk with power, that it has somehow absorbed not the lessons of prudent realists such as George Kennan, but the spirit of the Athenian generals who, Thucydides tells us, informed the Melians that, between the strong and the weak, only the language of power matters. It seems futile to recall from the history of empire that even when imperialism imposes direct rule it is always threatened by rebellions and rising costs. Moreover, the shrinking of democracy at home does not go well with the spread of democracy abroad.

Perhaps it is also futile to say that in occupied Iraq the best advice would suggest what not to do: don't hand-pick favorites who will be discredited; don't allow the men in the "deck of cards" to be tried by a purely American instead of an international court; don't appoint or select American companies to rewrite the history textbooks for young Iraqis or to exploit the oil fields. In foreign policy, following norms of self-restraint and international law and institutions can augment the real power of a strong country even if such norms curb the harshest uses of military power. The anti-Americanism on the rise throughout the world is not just hostility toward the most powerful nation, or based on the old clichés of the left and the right; nor is it only envy or hatred of our values. It is, more often than not, a resentment of double standards and double talk, of crass ignorance and arrogance, of wrong assumptions and dubious policies. Whether our current leaders are capable of self-examination at a time of military victory may affect the planet for a long time to come.

—May 15, 2003

FOOTNOTES

1 It was not a journalist, but the dean of the Woodrow Wilson School at Princeton, Anne-Marie Slaughter, who revealed in *The Washington Post* on April 13, 2003, that the French ambassador to Washington had relayed to the administration a French proposal that could have avoided the bitter Franco-American break: the US would have given up the idea of proposing a second resolution (which it finally had to withdraw since there weren't enough votes for it), and France and the US would have "agreed to disagree." This would have made the threat of a French veto unnecessary, and allowed the US to proceed with its war and to invoke Resolution 1441 as a basis for it. But Bush preferred a public showdown on a second resolution which Tony Blair needed at home. It preferred helping Blair, a loyal ally, to a deal with Chirac, a dissenting and thus lapsed ally.

2 The sanctions part of this containment policy did, however, hurt the Iraqi public—mainly children—without much affecting the regime.

3 The new policy of the administration is to substitute ad hoc "coalitions of the willing," led by Washington, for established institutions. (One such coalition may be a force composed of pro-US Europeans under Polish command, aimed at helping US and British forces to "stabilize" Iraq.)

4 See my "The High and the Mighty," *The American Prospect*, January 13, 2003.

5 See the exegesis of the new strategic doctrine by Philip Zelikow, "The Transformation of National Security," *The National Interest*, Spring 2003.

6 David C. Hendrickson, "Preserving the Imbalance of Power," *Ethics and International Affairs*, Vol. 17, No. 1 (2003), pp. 157–162.

7 John Brady Kiesling, "Diplomatic Breakdown," *The Boston Globe Magazine*, April 27, 2003.

8 See Minxin Pei, "The Paradoxes of American Nationalism," *Foreign Policy*, May/June 2003, pp. 30–37. I made similar points long ago, in *Gulliver's Troubles, or The Setting of American Foreign Policy* (McGraw-Hill, 1968), pp. 102 ff.

9 See Eli J. Lake, "Split Decision," and Kanan Makiya, "The Wasteland," in *The New Republic*, May 5, 2003.

10 See Owen R. Cote Jr., "Weapons of Mass Confusion," *Boston Review*, April/May 2003.

11 See Samantha Power, *"A Problem from Hell": America and the Age of Genocide* (Basic Books, 2002).

IRAQ: THE TRAP AND THE WAY OUT

THE LAST PARAGRAPH OF THE EARLIER ANALYSIS, written around the time President Bush proclaimed "mission accomplished" on an aircraft carrier, contained more than a grain of skepticism. Doubt turned out to be justified. As of the summer of 2004, Iraq is still occupied, security has not been restored, many public services remain battered, and the re-creation of a legitimate political process is still in limbo. Iraq has so far been both an embarrassment and a trap for the Bush administration. It is an embarrassment because the most widely used arguments for the invasion—Saddam's weapons of mass destruction and his collusion with al-Qaeda—have been proven false. (We are still waiting for the congressional investigation of the intelligence provided to the US government to tell us whether or not false information was partly the result of the administration's own pressure on the intelligence agencies; but it appears obvious that terrorism has received a boost from the invasion.) The administration's venture in Iraq appears more and more like a huge kick into a poisoned ant hill, and all the options seem grim.

IT IS CERTAIN THAT IRAQ IS NOT VIETNAM—the US does not confront the North Vietnamese army in addition to the Vietcong. A moderately "happy end" is not completely to be ruled out—but we find once again very familiar flaws: wrong assumptions, immoderate and confused ends, served by a mixture of counterproductive, inadequate, mismanaged, and, at times, scandalous means. Everything that the Bush administration had assumed about the postwar situation turned out to be false. Indeed, as soon as Baghdad fell, the Americans understood that they were not greeted everywhere as liberators, as Paul Wolfowitz and many others among the neoconservatives had predicted. In addition, they underestimated the armed resistance of elements of the Baath Party and of members of the Republican Guard, dispersed in Iraq and particularly in the Sunni Triangle. The Pentagon had carefully prepared the quick return of the exiles, but they put themselves out in front too quickly, and discovered that they were not very popular. Why this quasi-total support for the Iraqi National Congress, the main body of exiles? Probably because their boss, Ahmad

1.

THE
TRAP

Chalabi, endorsed the great ambition of the civilians at the Pentagon to reorganize the whole Arab world, and seemingly offered the best chance for placing Iraq in the American orbit. As for the goals of the war, both Bush and Blair have had to go through quaint contortions in order to argue that Saddam's regime did indeed represent a major security threat for the US and the world, or could have become one again—the former argument being hard to believe, and the latter one stretching the case for preventive war far beyond credibility. They have therefore insisted more and more on what I would call a double humanitarian argument: they have, they say, liberated the Iraqis from a horrible tyranny, and they seek to establish a democratic and moderate Iraqi government. The removal of the tyrant has been an undeniable blessing surrounded by a mass of highly debatable legal justifications, and accomplished in a way that has, so far, left many Iraqis resentful. The goal of a democratic Iraq is even more controversial. Instant, or quasi-instant, democracy is not likely, in a country marked by so many cleavages—ethnic, religious, social; modern classes versus traditional status groups; diverse solidarities or political ideologies; "a conflictual space in which secularism competes with Islamism, centralism with federalism, traditional patriarchy with the emancipation of women, and liberalism with statism"[1]—and no experience of democracy. For the US to create, or assist in the creation of, the institutions and the practices democracy requires would mean a very long occupation, and the need to fight strongly motivated insurgents while doing it. This was not what the US faced in Germany and Japan in 1945. Moreover, ignorance of Iraq's past, of its culture and history, is widespread among American elites and forces. (One of the many merits of *Fahrenheit 9/11* is to show the clash of cultures between the young American soldiers and the traumatized Iraqis.)

Democracy does not come fast, nor does it come from the outside. The outsider breeds nationalism against him. As J. G. Herder wrote more than two centuries ago:

The happiness of one people cannot be imposed upon

any other.... The roses for the wreath of liberty must be picked by one's own hand, and they must have grown up joyfully out of their own needs, out of their own desires and love.... The yoke of an alien, badly introduced freedom would be a terrible nuisance for a foreign people.[2]

Before a democratic Iraq can develop, there is a need for a genuine civil society and for basic institutions at the local level—as well as an impartial judiciary and a responsible bureaucracy. In other words, democracy must come out of state-building, and this can best be helped by the UN and by the international community—not by the US alone.

But is a democratic Iraq really the objective of the Bush administration? The rather pitiful sums devoted, in the US budget, to nation-building in Afghanistan, and the lagging disbursement of funds for the recovery of Iraq, make one wonder. After all, a democratic Iraq may not support many of America's policies, especially in the Middle East. Majority rule may benefit Islamic Shiism, while a system aimed at protecting minorities may be resented and opposed by the Shiite majority. Isn't America's real objective a "friendly" Iraq? This is the best explanation for what has been called an attempt "not only to repair and selectively reform Iraq, but to virtually reinvent it—economically, socially, politically," thus displaying "a vision in which reform is conflated with foreign hegemony."[3] The prominent role given by the occupiers to Iraqi exiles with little support in the country but strong connections with the American intelligence services that financed them, the awarding of profitable contracts to American companies (such as, of course, Halliburton), the plans for establishing US military bases, the very size of the new American embassy and its branches in the country—all this goes far beyond a mere concern for preventing the reemergence of a dangerous Iraq. It also goes a long way toward explaining the shift among Iraqis from happiness at being relieved of Saddam's tyranny to disenchantment with the occupation and hostility toward it.

The confusion and proliferation of objectives result from

what I consider the original sins of the entire venture, which resemble those of the Vietnam War: ignorance of the local conditions, hubris about what the US can hope to accomplish, unawareness of "the foreignness of foreigners,"[4] and neglect of the warning of the nineteenth-century sociologist Auguste Comte. A contemporary of Tocqueville but philosophically far away from him, Comte famously wrote that "one only destroys what one replaces," and the US had no clear or effective design for replacement.

If we turn to the means, we can distinguish between mistakes and abuses. As soon as their victory was achieved, the GIs tried to turn themselves into soldiers of peace and the gap in planning for the postwar occupation became blindingly apparent. It would be incorrect to say that the Americans had not prepared anything. But the working groups that the State Department had constituted have had no influence, for several rather appalling reasons. On the one hand, the Iraqi exiles and especially Chalabi, the favorite of the Pentagon civilians, had promised the

Americans that much of the army and police of Saddam Hussein would change sides, as the Italians had in 1943, and furthermore that vast clandestine forces were ready to take over the maintenance of security. "Don't worry," they said to the Americans, "you shall be greeted as liberators." It was therefore not necessary to mobilize twenty or thirty thousand more soldiers. In any case, the military were unenthusiastic at the idea that they would be utilized for police functions, which was absolutely not what they had been trained for. On the other hand, even if there had been efforts to prepare the postwar situation, these efforts were handicapped by the disagreements between the State Department and the Defense Department, hence, a genuine cacophony. The Pentagon civilians prevailed and adopted the ideas of their clients, the exiles who wanted the liquidation of Saddam's army and the sacking of his bureaucracy, which was decided by the American proconsul Paul Bremer, left a void both for security and for reconstruction, and fueled the now unemployed Iraqis' resentments. Let us take the problem of looting. The Americans saw to it that the oil fields would be guarded, but why did they remain indifferent to all the other scenes of looting? A good number of curators of American and European museums had immediately launched an appeal to prevent the looting of the Iraqi museums. They were not listened to and the looting took place with the occupation forces looking on. This has had a disastrous effect on the morale of the Iraqis. The economic effects have been incalculable and have delayed the return to a more normal situation.

If the overthrow of the regime was a relatively easy thing, the restoration of order proved much more difficult. The Americans knew how to plan for military operations with great care but they had no experience of any sort in the management of Iraqi political and administrative affairs. They have been paying the price for this ever since. The relative failure of the postwar occupation is not the result of technical difficulties, of a lack of means: it is undeniably a political issue. Everybody agreed on the goal, the democratization of Iraq, but things were much more difficult once one had to decide how to achieve that, or how not to antagonize the Iraqi population. The ignorance of the culture, the habits, and the complexity of Iraqi society didn't exactly help. Americans, too sure of themselves, had underestimated the state of public opinion, even if the Iraqis had indeed been oppressed for a very long time.

The result of all this has been double. First, for the average urban Iraqi, insecurity, unknown under Saddam, has continued. Secondly, American forces have been subjected to many kinds of attacks: the number of deaths since the end of operations has far exceeded that of soldiers killed during the military operations; also, within the first five months, there have been spectacular attacks against oil fields and pipelines, against the headquarters of the United Nations, against the main Shiite mosques, etc., etc. The objective of those attacks was less to kill people than to increase insecurity and to delay the process of economic reconstruction of the country. They have often been attributed to infiltrations of terrorists, al-Qaeda or groups affiliated with al-Qaeda, but there have also been attacks by Iraqi civilians exasperated by the often brutal control exerted by American soldiers. Thus one got to an absurd situation: war had been declared in the name of the world struggle against terrorism, and victory has favored the installation of terrorism in Iraq.

I must repeat: the confusion has not been only over material issues but also over politics. Was it necessary to begin by imposing almost total American and British control over the country in order to purge the Baathists, including in the police and administration? Wouldn't it have been better to follow the road the first head of the occupation, General Jay Garner, chosen by the Pentagon, had seemed to want to open, to awaken quickly new political forces, beginning at the local level, so that it would have been Iraqis recruiting an Iraqi police force for the urgent tasks such as security and the fight against terrorists? This would also have raised tough questions. While those political forces got organized, should one have given broad leeway to the Iraqis, or should one have warned them against giving any power to Shiite Islamists or to the former leaders of tribes? Some have evoked the German and Japanese precedents of 1945 but the resemblances are few; there was neither a homogeneous and docile population, as in Japan, nor were there liberal, socialist, and Catholic traditions, which had played an important role in Germany in the nineteenth century, and dominated under the Weimar Republic. Iraq is a country where political life had been totally repressed, where relations between the Shiites, the majority of the population whom Saddam had oppressed, and the Sunni, who were in a minority and whom Saddam had favored, were extremely tense; where the Kurds had, since 1991, succeeded in acquiring an almost complete autonomy with a sort of two-party system but only thanks to America's protection. Finally, there were the exiles, financed and used by the Pentagon and security agencies. General Garner had supported the exiles, talked about a provisional government, and held a few preparatory meetings, but in a rather confused manner. Above all, in the face of events, he did not seem to have sufficient weight. Hence his replacement in May 2003 by a diplomat, Paul Bremer, a former aide to Henry Kissinger, who was acceptable both to the State Department, which had been quite frustrated under Garner, and to the Pentagon, but he had no experience in the Arab world. His arrival meant a kind of recapture of control, priority for problems of security in daily life, extreme reliance (which reminded one of McNamara in the Vietnam days) on statistics of material progress, and the postponement of political renewal. He also made the mistake of demobilizing Iraq's army and of purging the Baathist administration. He did, it is true, constitute an interim governmental authority, but it has had very little authority. It was kept on a short leash by its American protectors; it was deeply divided; it had a small majority of former exiles; and it was not capable of obtaining the UN's blessing.

There was an awakening of awareness to the situation in the United States, both in public opinion and in the media; members of Congress worried greatly about security issues and, above all, about the cost the President finally announced: $87 billion for Iraq and Afghanistan, $67 of which were for the armed struggle. The military at the

Pentagon asked for additional forces to be sent to Iraq, which would have made the American army capable of preserving security in the cities, chasing the terrorists, protecting the borders, and serving as a police and battle force. But Rumsfeld has obstinately refused. Was it because he didn't want the armed forces to get bogged down in a new Vietnam? Or was it because he wanted to keep substantial forces for other possible conflicts? Was it in order to ensure that his gamble about "slimming down" the mammoth American army could be won? The military around him could grumble, but did not dare contradict him. Congress, which of course has been thinking about the elections of 2004, did not like sending more troops either, on the whole. Under those conditions, what is there to be done? The solution, which some have mentioned, of attempting aggressively to hire and train police forces and a new Iraqi army proved far from effective. It would have meant, as usual, giving priority to the urgent over the long-term, which was the reconstitution of an Iraqi authority that would control these forces. However, in the absence of such an authority, they inevitably had to be placed under American and British command and were treated as the coalition's auxiliaries by many Iraqis. To resolve in such a way the numerical problem of forces—on paper and for an uncertain length of time—without any movement on the political ground was not really satisfactory. By the fall of 2003 the political problem had still not been solved; the Sunnis have been hostile, and the Shiites have been divided between pro-Americans and a young Islamist clergy which rejects the occupation.

As for the other frequently mentioned idea of calling on new members for the coalition, such as India, Thailand, Turkey, France, Germany, etc., it raised two major problems. From a strictly military viewpoint, the American high command and also Rumsfeld were not very well disposed; it would have complicated the exercise of command, confronting again, as in Kosovo, the difficulties characteristic of coalitions, and diluted the authority of the American high commanders. Finally and above all, some of the eventual partners made it clear that in exchange for the "right" of sharing with the present coalition the losses and the expenses, they wanted a resolution from the Security Council which would have enlarged the role of the United Nations and defined the framework of this new coalition, indicated its objectives, and given the UN a right of supervision. (Kofi Annan did not ask for more; he did not want to send blue-helmeted soldiers into a war zone, but he didn't want less either.) This has for a long time been unacceptable to American hawks, who have not forgotten the confusion of the double chain of command (the UN and the US) in Bosnia, and above all did not want to appear to capitulate before an organization which had not supported them at the decisive moment—an organization which they deplore. Colin Powell, on whom all difficult tasks are pushed, tried to find a compromise formula, with the agreement of the President. Once again France was particularly reluctant and asked for a primary role for the UN, a return, so to speak, to international legitimacy. In any case, an enlargement of the coalition meant complicating the work of the Anglo-American authority which the

Security Council recognized but did not legitimize, and it meant multiplying targets for terrorists, who saw enemies in the partners of the Americans and did not hesitate to kill their representatives and those of the UN even when they were engaged in humanitarian work; this was probably a memory of the bitter years of sanctions inflicted on Iraq by the United Nations.

In fact, American diplomats have, since the fall of 2003, looked for a squaring of the circle: the creation of a multinational force, of a broader coalition sponsored by the UN but under American command. This meant the continuation of the ineffective power of the interim governing authority, with a legitimation by the UN which it has not been possible to achieve fully. Indeed, the main obstacle to the success of this attempt was Bush himself, supported by Dick Cheney and Donald Rumsfeld. He continued imperturbably to speak about a universal war against terrorism, to call for total victory, and to make Iraq the central battlefield in this struggle. In order to invite other countries to cooperate with the coalition within the framework of the

UN and for the good of the Iraqis, he has summoned these countries to participate, in the interest of humankind, in this struggle and in the sharing of burdens with the United States, but not in the sharing of responsibilities. If American forces were not increased, it was evident that sooner or later they would have to be relieved of everything but the restoration of security, and the US would have to accept a return to the UN both in order to facilitate nation-building, i.e., reconstruction, an area in which the UN has long experience, and above all to revive political life in a country which has never had one. A dubious coalition is not best placed for the promotion of democracy and liberalism. Some time ago, there had been a failed "Vietnamization"; what was needed now was an "Iraqization" under international guidance.

The confusions of the search for a political course continued: Paul Bremer ended up retreating from his policy of total debaathification, less because it had produced hundreds of thousands of now unemployed foes of the occupation than because of the need to rebuild security forces against the insurgents, and to reinstate technicians for the repair of basic services. Then Washington decided on the transfer of (some) sovereignty to a new interim government—something Bremer had not appeared to favor. This group was provided with a temporary constitution that proved to be a bone of contention between Shiites and Kurds, the Shiites making it clear that they would not permanently accept the privileged position of the Kurds. But even though the administration had appeared to turn to the UN for the selection of the members of the new government, and even though the UN representative had expressed his intention to select technocrats (probably so as not to prejudge the results of the elections scheduled for the end of 2004), the US interfered in the process and insisted on the inclusion of political figures. It chose as head of the interim government Iyad Allawi, a man who was not the UN candidate but a former employee of the CIA. This almost guaranteed a lack of legitimacy of the new "rulers" in the eyes of suspicious Iraqis. Moreover, the transfer of power was bound to remain limited, since the

US insisted on retaining control of military operations (with the interim government being, at most, consulted), and even objected to the scope of the amnesty planned by the prime minister, wanting to exclude from it killers of Americans—a discrimination that killed the project.

There were also confused and contradictory attitudes toward insurgent forces that remain both intense and mysterious. Declarations of war on the rebels of Falluja, in the Sunni Triangle, and on the young Shiite cleric Moqtada al-Sadr were followed by prudent retreats, since the attempts at killing or capturing the enemy would have been devastating for the civilian population. The US encouraged the Iraqi authorities to recruit and train security forces, but the many private militias remain in place, despite calls for their dissolution.

Throughout the occupation, the US has overestimated Iraq's capacity for fast reconstruction and a quick return to security, and it has underestimated both the strength of internal antagonisms and the funds needed to rebuild the country. Oil revenues remain far below expectations, partly because of sabotage and insecurity, partly because of large payments to American companies. In view of the time needed to train Iraqi security forces, and the reluctance of their members to confront Iraqi rebels on behalf of the occupiers, it became obvious that fewer than 140,000 coalition troops would not be adequate. But given Rumsfeld's determination to keep the numbers down (while saying that if the military asked for more he would give them what they wanted—but also making it clear that he was not encouraging them to ask), the Pentagon had to resort to a variety of measures to prolong the stay of many American troops, thus increasing the unpopularity of the war with families at home. The proportion of men and women drawn from the National Guard and Reserves is now around 40 percent. If, as Michael Ignatieff has written, nation-building in Afghanistan was "nation-building lite," the occupation has been carried out by a military presence not exactly cheap (since new funds have become necessary) but meager with respect to the tasks facing it. This has put on the current interim government a burden it is not well equipped to bear or legitimate enough to handle well. With insecurity disrupting daily life and resulting in huge casualties among civilians, continuing feuding about a meeting aimed at providing the Iraqi executive with a consultative assembly, and several cities in the insurgents' hands, the plans and schedule for national elections by the end of 2004 appear shaky.

Another feature of the occupation has been a high degree of confusion in the chain of command. It was not always evident that Paul Bremer had full final authority over the military. Nor was it evident that the commander of the coalition forces exerted full control over his subordinates, over the military police, and, above all, over the intelligence bodies. (When senators, especially John McCain, asked the secretary of defense to explain the chain of command, he turned to the military officers accompanying him; they did not provide him with a clear answer.) Interservice rivalries did not end. The marine commanders often boasted of having a better understanding of Iraqi concerns than the army. The feud, on the one hand, between the Pentagon and its intelligence suppliers, and on the other, the CIA, exploded in the spectacular raid of Iraqi forces, escorted by CIA agents, against Chalabi, the Pentagon's candidate for leadership. The CIA argued that the controversial Chalabi had provided important information to Iran (not to mention the misinformation he had abundantly provided to the US).[5] The new head of the interim government, Iyad Allawi, was the CIA's man. Chalabi had received more than $300,000 a month until April, and the Pentagon's unhappiness at his demise was forcefully expressed by Richard Perle.

Much of all this was the consequence of the initial unpreparedness and ignorance; some of it was a rather startling display of incompetence—startling because of the discipline the administration had observed in its stealthy march to war and during the brief war against Saddam. This incompetence extended to a kind of blindness to the symbolic effects of US policies: after the failure of the US to protect against the looting of museums and hospitals came George W. Bush's promise to build a new central prison for the new sovereign Iraq, and of course, the Abu Ghraib affair in Saddam's former house of torture.

This brings us to the abuse of prisoners. Some cases were finally dealt with by the Supreme Court (which, however, left standing the bizarre category of "enemy combatants"). Many provisions of the Patriot Act remain to be tested in courts. One of the most extraordinary affairs is the attempt by Pentagon lawyers to argue that the president's "commander-in-chief authority" allows him to do whatever he deems required for the protection of the US—including authorizing torture. (The administration had already decided not to apply the Geneva Conventions to prisoners in Afghanistan, nor to enforce the conventions against torture and other cruel, inhuman, and degrading treatment or punishment.[6])

This was part of the background to the cruel, inhuman, and degrading practices that were used at Abu Ghraib. From the Red Cross protests of 2003 to the revelations of the spring of 2004, there is enough evidence to show that these horrific acts were not just carried out by a few "rotten apples" in a barrel. As one psychologist put it, they were the product of the barrel itself; nor were they limited to one prison. There have been reports of torture at several other places in Iraq and Afghanistan. It is clear that at Abu Ghraib military intelligence officers had pushed aside the prison's commander, and that the high command both failed to take seriously reports that described violations and to intervene forcefully in the places where they were committed. That the investigations ordered by the army resulted in a whitewash was not surprising since self-investigation is rarely a guarantee of justice. So far, only low-level soldiers and guards have been indicted or con-demned—a fact that has only strengthened the catastrophic effect the pictures from Abu Ghraib have had, not only in the Muslim world, but everywhere else.

Other abuses are the almost inevitable results of coun-terinsurgency actions by forces that are not equipped, materially or psychologically, for a kind of warfare that aims at avoiding or minimizing "collateral damage." From brutal intrusions into suspects' homes to air strikes that kill indiscriminately innocent civilians and suspects, such actions have done a great deal to foster either outright hostility or increased support for the insurgents (as long as they themselves do not kill Iraqis indiscriminately). This problem is one of many that illustrate the American dilemma in Iraq. US moderation in the form of some tacit accommodation with insurgents and resisters leaves them in at least partial control. All-out assaults on them play into their hands, insofar as popular support is concerned. Both approaches have been tried in Falluja and Najaf.

A last form of abuse is a practice that is beginning to attract attention—the "outsourcing," or privatization, of war-related activities. The problem with entrusting what used to be public responsibilities to private, profit-seeking entrepreneurs—American and foreign—is partly (but only partly) caused by the need to keep the size of US forces down. (The foreign enterprises have proven easier to blackmail out of Iraq, through kidnappings and beheadings, than the American ones.) This practice results in a high degree of irresponsibility. The employees of these private operations are answerable only to their bosses, not to the military or to the official US bureaucrats who employ them. This has been one factor in the Abu Ghraib debacle. In the 1990s, the CIA "outsourced the Iraq project"—aimed at "creating the conditions for the removal of Saddam Hussein from power," as instructed by the first President Bush—to a firm specializing in "perception management," the Rendon Group, which "was charged with the delicate task of helping to create a viable and united opposition movement against Saddam." The CIA used Chalabi for this purpose, continuing to support him until 1996.[7] One of the most striking aspects of the administration's attitude toward its mistakes and abuses has been the apparent immunity of all those responsible. (The 9/11 Commission, determined to present a unanimous report, has preferred spreading blame to specifying it.) Except for George Tenet, nobody has resigned; and nobody has been publicly fired.

WHAT IS TO BE DONE? There are many who believe that the US has to "stay the course," and that—especially after having failed to support various insurrections against Saddam, in 1991 after the Gulf War and in Kurdistan in 1996 —American "credibility" is at stake. Moreover, especially among Republican supporters, the mirage of democracy for Iraq and the entire region, and the desire for a reliable Iraq, have been combined in arguments for helping not only the interim government to defeat the insurgencies but also the one that would emerge from the forthcoming election. The spread of terrorism in Iraq makes it difficult to sort out Islamist terrorists from outside the country, or Iraqi postwar affiliates of Osama bin Laden, from Iraqi insurgents against the occupation with their own political aims. Thus, the "war against terrorism" that has become an American priority and obsession has been achieving the very amalgamation between Iraq and al-Qaeda that the administration had falsely denounced. Others point out that the prolonged occupation "is an open invitation for a steady buildup of grassroots Muslim anger,"[8] and a

2.
THE
WAY
OUT

breeding ground for terrorism in a country where, under Saddam, the official use of terror was strictly aimed at Iraqis disloyal to him.

At present, much of the insurgency is not aimed principally at the American occupiers but at oil pipelines and at deterring other members of the coalition—private entrepreneurs from abroad, and ordinary technicians and Iraqis—from working for and with the Americans. It may well be that many Iraqis currently disgruntled with the occupation will be increasingly revolted by the killings of Iraqis by the insurgents and by the insecurity they foster. In this case, an official campaign to repress the insurgents may become popular or at least accepted. But as long as such a policy needs the muscular support of American forces, it also risks being caught in a trap. Those who, especially among the Democrats, call on NATO or on other foreign troops to join the American and British forces and thus to help stabilize Iraq and its new institutions need to realize that this is less a solution—even if such forces receive a UN mandate—than wishful thinking. Those

NATO countries that favored the "coalition" are already (or—in Spain's case—were) in it. France and Germany are very unlikely to provide sizable forces; the French concern with not giving to the Muslim world the image of "the West versus Islam" will not vanish. As for Muslim countries, they have shown no enthusiasm for helping Iraqi authorities as long as the "coalition" is still under US control. Others may come in, either to help train Iraqi forces, or to join them, but only if the Americans leave.

There are good reasons for calling for the end of the occupation. As in Palestine, the occupation is the main cause of the current troubles (which does not mean that the troubles will end if we leave; but whatever we do to try to resolve the internal conflicts is likely to backfire). Continuing US military control, direct or indirect, will feed anti-Americanism (as in post-1965 South Vietnam) and provide a training and breeding ground for terrorism, native and from other countries. American interests would be better served by a shift of US resources toward two major tasks. The first is the fight against al-Qaeda and its allies around the world—who have become more diversi-fied and decentralized and continue to receive manpower and support from schools and factions in officially pro-American states such as Saudi Arabia and Pakistan. The sec-ond would be a much more extensive program aimed at rebuilding the economic infrastructure of Iraq and at help-ing to establish new institutions with the partnership of other states experienced in state-building.

The exit of American and British forces would make it easier for countries that have not supported the war to provide assistance (including police training) under UN auspices. Advocates of eventual withdrawal have argued convincingly that "a permanent [US] military garrison in Iraq" would "impose enormous costs and a host of new headaches for the American taxpayers and the military alike," and that the American military presence in Iraq con-tributes "to a worsening perception of the United States by a growing number of Muslims" (and, I would add, non-Muslims).[9] It is time to refocus the struggle against terror-ism, by giving priority to the fight against Islamic jihadists (the most dangerous for US and Western interests), and by spending far more energy on a permanent solution to the Palestinian problem, along the lines almost agreed upon at Taba in 2001 and advocated by the informal Geneva alliance of Palestinians and Israelis, as well as by Jimmy Carter.

What would such an exit strategy mean, concretely? It would require a statement by the coalition of its intention to withdraw its forces by a certain date: let us say, within six months of the establishment of a newly elected assembly and the government that emanates from it, and no later than the end of June 2005. During the period of the present interim government, the US would take measures that have genuine political and symbolic significance: a "normalization" of the size and nature of the US embassy, the elimination of formal US advisers in the ministries, granting the Iraqi government the right to ask for military operations, a commitment not to launch any such operations unless they are so requested, and the removal of the US from the preparation and supervision of the coming elections. These elections should be left to the UN, which could cancel or replace the decisions by commissions set up by Bremer to determine eligibility to vote. (Only the certifiable criminals of the Baath army and bureaucracy ought to be excluded, as well as terrorists condemned for their actions.) During this period, the training of Iraqi security forces might, of necessity, remain a task for the coalition, but it ought to be monitored and supervised by the UN.

After the Iraqi elections, the withdrawal of coalition forces would begin. They would be replaced by Iraqis and by the forces of any country—including the US and the UK—that is acceptable by the Iraqis and agrees to participate in an international peacemaking and peacekeeping force set up with the consent of the new Iraqi government and placed under the control of the UN. The command would be Iraqi. The new government would have the right to renegotiate the contracts awarded by the coalition, to have full control of the oil revenues, and to decide on a permanent status for the oil industry. No foreign bases would be established in Iraq.

Such a policy might be more of a source of embarrassment for anti-American insurgents and terrorists than an opportunity. They could no longer argue that Iraq is an American outpost with a government chosen by Washington. If they continue their fight, and if it can be shown that an increasingly large number among them are from outside Iraq, they would risk unifying Iraq's new political forces and peoples against them. Successful counterinsurgency requires popular support, and foreign occupation inhibits such support. Conversely, the longer the occupation remains in Iraq, the more difficult it will be for the occupiers to extricate themselves. It is particularly important that the US allow the Iraqis to decide on the nature of their future government, and on the substance of their new permanent constitution.

No doubt the course advocated here entails risks. A breakup of the country because of its multiple lines of national and religious identity is by no means to be ruled out. A policy of withdrawal could lead to a civil war, or to foreign interventions, say, by Iran helping Iraqi Shiite clerics, or by Turkey trying to prevent Kurdish secession. These risks partly explained why the first Bush administration was so reluctant to intervene in the domestic affairs of Iraq. But preventing a bloody disintegration of Iraq and preventing a takeover by Islamic extremist terrorists, in case new Iraqi security forces do not suffice, ought to be left to international diplomacy by the UN and regional organizations such as NATO, as well as to international peacemaking forces provided by them.

Would such an American policy be one of defeatism and weakness? It should be clear that remaining trapped among equally unpromising choices would weigh heavily on US foreign policy in general. (General de Gaulle had understood this would be a consequence for France in the case of Algeria, and suggested to the US, in vain, that the same outcome could be expected in Indochina.) On the other hand, Americans will be able to argue that they helped Iraq decisively by eliminating Saddam (at a heavy cost in international support and prestige), that they gave Iraq back to its people, that it is now up to the Iraqis to make a success or a mess out of it with international help whenever it is needed. The best the US can still do is not to fight within the vicious circle of a counterinsurgency war, but to shift resources toward aid for reconstruction and development, as well as to take part in genuinely international peacemaking and peacekeeping if the Iraqis call for American participation.

Nothing wholly good can come out of a war that resulted from a mix of self-deception and deliberate deception, waged in a part of the world in which alien control has for a long time fostered turmoil and tragedy. The presence of terrorism is not an invitation to empire, but an incentive for finding policies that reduce its appeal, and for pursuing the terrorists in ways that do not help them multiply. In the case of the Middle East, an exit from Iraq, combined with a new effort by the US, the UN, the EU, and Russia to end the Israeli occupation of Palestinian lands and to create a livable Palestinian state, would mark a return to reality, to good sense, and to morality.

—*September 9, 2004*

STANLEY HOFFMANN

FOOTNOTES

1 See Faleh A. Jabar, *Postconflict Iraq*, Special Report #120, US Institute of Peace, May 2004.

2 See Ioannis D. Evrigenis and Daniel Pellerin, *Johann Gottfried Herder—Another Philosophy of History* (Hackett, 2004), Part V.

3 Carl Conetta, Radical Departure: *Toward a Practical Peace in Iraq*, Project on Defense Alternatives Briefing Report #16, July 8, 2004, at the Commonwealth Institute, Cambridge, Massachusetts.

4 I used this expression in *Gulliver's Troubles* (McGraw Hill, 1968).

5 See Jane Mayer, "The Manipulator," *The New Yorker*, June 7, 2004, pp. 58–72; and Thomas Powers, in Mark Follman, "A Temporary Coup," at archive.salon .com/news/feature/2004/06/14/coup/index_np.html. If Chalabi did indeed serve Iranian interests, the Iranians will have brilliantly succeeded in a double whammy: they have gotten the Americans to get rid of their enemy Saddam Hussein and to remain stuck in Iraq, which deters any likely attack on Iran.

6 See the *Working Group Report on Detainee Interrogations in the Global War on Terrorism*, March 6, 2003; and Anthony Lewis, "Making Torture Legal," *The New York Review of Books*, July 15, 2004, pp. 4–8.

7 Mayer, "The Manipulator," pp. 61–62.

8 Christopher Preble, *Exiting Iraq*, report of a special task force sponsored by the Cato Institute, 2004, p. 30.

9 Preble, *Exiting Iraq*, p. 17.

The New York Review of Books

The New York Review of Books, published twenty times each year, has been called "the country's most successful intellectual journal." (*The New York Times*)

To find out more, including how to subscribe, visit our website: www.nybooks.com. Or call or write:

The New York Review of Books
1755 Broadway
New York, New York 10019
Telephone: (212) 757-8070
Fax: (212) 333-5374
Email: nyrsub@nybooks.com